The Extraordinary Life of Anna Swan

Anne Renaud

CAPE BRETON UNIVERSITY PRESS
SYDNEY, NOVA SCOTIA

Cape Breton University Press recognizes the support of Canada Council for the Arts and of the Province of Nova Scotia, through the Department of Communities, Culture and Heritage. We are pleased to work in partnership with these bodies to develop and promote our cultural resources.

Cover Images: Front, Anna and Martin, courtesy of the Creamery Square Heritage Centre, poster insert see page 24; back, see page 30; title page, Anna Swan, courtesy of Laddy Kite.
Cover design: Gail Jones, Sydney, NS
Layout: Gail Jones, Sydney, NS
First printed in Canada

Library and Archives Canada Cataloguing in Publication

Renaud, Anne, 1957-

The extraordinary life of Anna Swan / Anne Renaud.
Includes bibliographical references and index.
ISBN 978-1-927492-37-6

1. Swan, Anna, 1846-1888--Juvenile literature. 2. Giants--Nova Scotia--Biography--Juvenile literature. I. Title.

GN69.22.S9R45   2013 j599.9'49   C2013-901291-5

Cape Breton University Press
PO Box 5300
Sydney, NS B1P 6L2
Canada

Table of Contents

Introduction

Did you hear?"

"Can it be?"

"Who would have thought . . . ?"

Across the rolling, green hills of Colchester County, news travelled fast throughout the farming community of Millbrook, Nova Scotia.

The year was 1846, and on the balmy morning of August 6, a child had been born to Ann and Alexander Swan in the couple's small wood cabin. This in itself was not odd, as home was where babies were most often born in the mid-nineteenth century. What was surprising, however, was that the baby girl weighed in at a hefty 6 kilograms (13 pounds) – almost twice the size of an average newborn!

Her parents named her Anna, and she would grow to an astonishing size. However, despite the challenges of her physical attributes, Anna Swan's life unfolded as a rich and happy one, gifted with fame, wealth, world travel and, most notably, true love. This is her remarkable story.

1

Chapter 1

Early Years

Anna Swan thrived in her family's caring and loving farmhouse, and her childhood was joyful. At times, her parents certainly found life with Anna to be a challenge. This was not because of bad behaviour, but rather for her surprisingly rapid growth.

While still a baby, Anna outgrew her cradle, and her father had to build her a bed. But in no time it had to be lengthened, then lengthened again. Anna's mattress and pillows, which were made of cotton fabric stuffed with straw and feathers from chickens and geese, were re-sized and re-stuffed so she could sleep comfortably. As for her clothing, Anna's mother could barely keep up with knitting and sewing clothes for her young daughter. Even Anna's shoes, which she outgrew at lightning pace, had little wear before the shoemaker had to make her a bigger pair.

At four years old, Anna already stood at 1.4 metres (4 feet 6 inches)!

Anna's parents were of average height, as were all the other Swan children. These included the two children born before Anna, who had sadly died in infancy, as well as the ten more children who would follow over the years. This made Anna's size all the more unusual.

When Anna was still a young child, her family moved from Millbrook to a new farmhouse in nearby New Annan, and though this wooden cabin was more comfortable than their previous home, life on the farm was still rugged. With no indoor plumbing, **chamber pots** and outhouses were used for toilets, and water for cooking and bathing was drawn from an outdoor well.

Anna's parents' home. Photo courtesy of the Creamery Square Heritage Centre.

Anna's parents toiled from early morning until dusk – milking cows, feeding chickens, ploughing fields, weeding vegetable gardens and cutting and raking hay – to provide for the family's needs. All the while Anna spent her days content, helping her parents with small household chores and playing with her dolls and younger siblings. As Anna grew in size, so did the Swan family, with the arrival of more babies.

In time, the curious and the nosy began making their way to the Swan farmhouse to catch a glimpse of the pink-cheeked

Anna's parents. Photo courtesy of the Creamery Square Heritage Centre.

girl who towered over her sisters and brothers, for Anna did indeed appear much older than her age.

This was the assumption once made by a stranger who came to the Swan farm to buy some cattle. Upon witnessing four year-old Anna sitting on the floor playing with her dolls, the man concluded she was a grown woman and therefore had to be a **Haftie** – a rather cruel expression.

Anna's father was quick to set the stranger straight on this account and, to ensure there were no hard feelings, invited the man to have dinner with the Swan family. It was during the course of this meal that the stranger convinced Anna's parents that people would be willing to pay money to see

their child, and they should
show her off in cities and
towns across Nova Scotia.

As a result, in March 1851,
Anna's parents brought
their four-and-a-half-year-
old daughter to Halifax, where she was put on exhibition.
Anna was a popular attraction and crowds of people were
eager to pay to see the "Infant Giantess" who was rosy as
a milkmaid, weighed more than 42 kilograms (94 pounds)
and already had arms and wrists as large as a full-grown
man, as she was described in a local newspaper. This
first appearance led to several others, with Anna and her
parents travelling from town to town for small county fairs,
where she could be featured. Anna's parents welcomed
the extra money that these appearances generated, as it
supplemented their meagre income as farmers. However,
they always made sure Anna was well cared for and the
touring was not too tiring for her.

At six years old Anna measured 1.6 metres, 5 centimetres
(5 feet, 4 inches) tall, surpassing her mother by 5
centimetres (2 inches) and standing eye-to-eye with her
father.

Anna had long looked forward to her first day of school,
but this new experience was met with sadness and
frustration. The other children teased her about her size,
and she was too big for her desk. But in time Anna's cheery

INFANT GIANTESS.—There is at present
exhibiting in Pictou a girl not five years of
age, who is 4 feet 8 inches in height, weighs
over 100 lbs. and is well proportioned. She
is accompanied by her mother—a woman of
small size, and interesting appearance.

The Nova Scotian,
July 14, 1851.

personality and sharp mind won her classmates over and the teasing stopped.

Determined to make his daughter as comfortable as possible at school, Anna's father raised her desk on wooden blocks, which allowed her to work while sitting on a high stool. Anna enjoyed school and took great pleasure in teaching her younger brothers and sisters all she learned. It was at this young age that she set her sights on becoming a teacher.

Anna and her parents. Photo courtesy of the Nova Scotia Museum.

At home, Anna's bed continued to be adjusted with every passing year, to accommodate her increasing frame. Eventually her bed was moved downstairs because the stairway had become too narrow for her. By the time Anna was a teenager she stood a little more than 2 metres (7 feet) tall. She had outgrown the family dinner table and no longer ate with her siblings. Rather, she sat on the floor with her back supported by the wall and had her meals at a table made especially for her.

As well, the constant stooping and banging into furniture made Anna's life uncomfortable and painful. Feeling clumsy and awkward indoors, she was most happy

outdoors, where she spent
much of her time exploring
the surrounding woods,
reading under a tree or
playing schoolteacher to
her younger siblings.

Original Normal School Building--Opened November 1855

Truro Normal School as it appeared when Anna attended. Courtesy of the Colchester Historical Society Museum and Archives.

Anna's thirst for knowledge eventually led her to Truro, where she moved in with one of her aunts and enrolled at the **Normal School** to become a schoolteacher. But Anna quickly grew unhappy for she could not escape the challenges she thought to have left behind in New Annan. Townsfolk were just as bothersome in Truro, in fact more so. When walking on the street she was constantly stopped and questioned about her height or even mocked. And while her aunt had her best interest at heart in providing her with a home while she pursued her studies, the house and all its furnishings were all much too small to accommodate Anna's size, as was the desk at the Normal School.

With a heavy heart, Anna gave up on her dream of becoming a schoolteacher and asked her father to come fetch her with his horse and wagon. Anna returned to New Annan, but it would not be long before she would take to the road once again, one which would lead to fame and fortune.

Chapter 2

Anna in New York

It was while Anna was studying in Truro that a **Quaker** who lived in nearby Pictou visited the office of Mr. P. T. Barnum in New York City and told him of a New Annan girl who measured more than 2 metres (7 feet) tall. Ever the shrewd businessman, Barnum realized that by hiring Anna, he would have the bragging rights to having a female giant as one of his star attractions. He quickly dispatched one of his agents to Nova Scotia to investigate the claims and to offer Anna a contract to appear in his American Museum.

Anna's parents did not welcome the prospect of having their 17-year-old daughter living so far away in a bustling city. But Anna saw Barnum's offer as a chance to further her education and earn a living for herself. By the time Barnum's agent made his third visit to New Annan, Anna had managed to convince her parents to let her join Barnum in New York and be put on display in his museum.

P. T. Barnum's American Museum was a combination zoo, art gallery, aquarium, concert hall and museum, which housed a collection of what were called at the time "curiosities" and "human oddities." After paying the 25-cent entrance fee, patrons could see any number of sights. At various times, Barnum had on display jugglers, **contortionists**, giants, midgets, wax figures, fossils and stuffed and live animals, including a rhinoceros, a hippopotamus, grizzly bears and snakes.

Phineas Taylor Barnum (1819-1891) was a world famous showman, entertainer and circus owner. Courtesy of the author.

The American Museum was open 15 hours a day and attracted thousands of visitors daily. Courtesy of the New York Public Library Digital Collection.

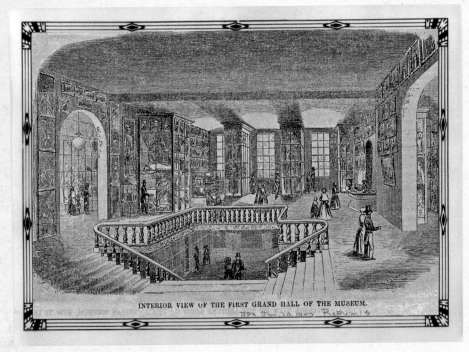

INTERIOR VIEW OF THE FIRST GRAND HALL OF THE MUSEUM.

Interior view of the first grand hall of the American Museum, 1853. Courtesy of the New York Public Library Digital Collection.

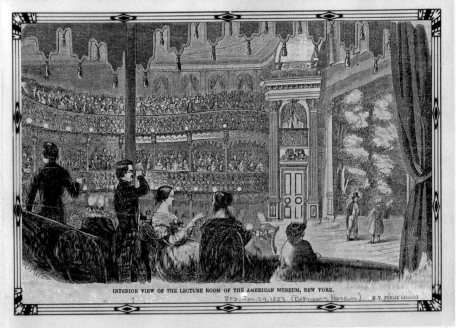

INTERIOR VIEW OF THE LECTURE ROOM OF THE AMERICAN MUSEUM, NEW YORK.

Interior view of the lecture room of the American Museum, New York, 1853. Courtesy of the New York Public Library Digital Collection.

Before a contract was signed, however, Anna's parents insisted that Barnum agree to a few conditions. Anna was to be provided with a private **tutor** for three hours every day for three years so she could continue her studies in music and literature, as well as be given singing and acting lessons. This person was also to act as Anna's **chaperone**, as it was not appropriate for a young lady to be without one at that time. As well, it was agreed that Anna's mother would remain with her in New York for a year, until she turned eighteen.

Once reassured their daughter would be treated with kindness and respect, Ann and Alexander Swan gave their permission. Filled with both fear and excitement, Anna packed her belongings and said goodbye to her friends and siblings. She and her parents then boarded a steamship in Halifax bound for New York, the city that was soon to become her new home.

By all accounts, Barnum was a fair and considerate employer and was said to be quite fond of Anna, describing her as an "intelligent and by no means ill-looking girl." Anna was paid a salary of $23 a week in gold – considered to be a small fortune at that time – and was provided with spacious living quarters within the museum, filled with oversized furniture. Barnum had beautiful clothing made especially for Anna and had her fitted with custom-made, size 16½ shoes and boots for her 33-centimetre (13-inch) feet. Barnum also had a carriage built for her, drawn by Clydesdale horses, in which Anna proudly rode around the city.

P. T. Barnum was a master of embellishment and exaggeration. He boasted in his promotional advertisements that Anna measured 2.46 metres (8 feet, 1 inch) in height. The truth, however, was that Anna's stature did not quite measure up to this claim, falling slightly short of 2.34 metres (8 feet). Barnum had Anna wear shoes with heels and style her hair atop her head to gain the extra height artificially.

Anna and a man of average height. Anna was said to have a goitre, which is quite visible in this photo. Courtesy of the Creamery Square Heritage Centre.

New York Times, *January 26, 1864*

Promotional card showing Anna and a woman of average height. Courtesy of Laddy Kite.

Anna was thrilled with her life in New York. Her many talents and gentle and cheery disposition made her a welcome and popular attraction at the museum, and she was greatly appreciated by both Barnum and his patrons. Her performances at the museum consisted mainly of playing the piano, giving lectures and poetry readings, participating in plays and **tableaux**, as well as conversing with many of the customers.

Medically, Anna most probably suffered from pituitary gigantism, which results in unusual height and size. This condition is caused by an excess of growth hormone, due to a pituitary adenoma, a type of brain tumour that affects the function of the pituitary gland. The pituitary gland is located at the base of the brain and is the master gland that controls other glands and influences numerous body functions including growth.

MISS ANNA SWAN,
Twenty years of age, EIGHT FEET HIGH, and weighing 413 pounds.

Promotional card showing Anna and two people of average height. Courtesy of Diane Gudatis.

Charles Sherwood Stratton was only four years old when P. T. Barnum "discovered" him in Bridgeport Connecticut in 1842. Measuring a mere 64 centimetres (25 inches) in height, Barnum renamed him General Tom Thumb and trained him to sing, dance, tell jokes and imitate famous people. Stratton performed at the American Museum and later toured the world, achieving great fame and wealth. In his teen years he began to grow again. When Stratton died in 1883 at the age of forty-six, he measured slightly more than 1 metre (40 inches).

General Tom Thumb and his wife Lavinia Warren. Courtesy of the author.

George Washington Morrison Nutt, to whom P. T. Barnum had given the stage name Commodore Nutt, was about 76 centimetres (30 inches) tall when he began performing at the American Museum. Barnum had a small carriage built for him, shaped like a nutshell, which was small enough for the Commodore to ride up on stage drawn by Shetland ponies. He was advertised as "The Smallest Man in the World" but later grew to a height of 1.1 metres (43 inches), 7 centimetres (3 inches) taller than General Tom Thumb's full height.

P. T. Barnum and Commodore Nutt. Courtesy of the Rail Splitter.

Although both Tom Thumb and Commodore Nutt were advertised by P. T. Barnum as dwarves, they were in fact midgets. The difference between the two is that midgets are perfectly proportioned human beings, only on a much smaller scale, while dwarves have normal upper bodies and stunted lower limbs.

Anna also made many friends with some of the other "human oddities" who were on display, including Joseph the French Giant, the Living Skeleton, General Tom Thumb and his wife Lavinia Warren and Commodore Nutt whom Barnum often paired with Anna to emphasize their differences in height.

Owing to their unusual physical attributes – which meant they were sometimes mocked or verbally abused by the general public – Anna and her museum friends formed a close-knit community where mutual respect and loyalty prevailed and no one was ever teased or ridiculed.

Despite the great distance between them, Anna's ties with her family back in New Annan also remained strong. She wrote home regularly, her letters filled with unusual sights and anecdotes of her intriguing life. Now earning a healthy income, Anna also included money with her letters to help her parents and brothers and sisters with family expenses. As well, Anna tried to visit them as often as she could.

Whenever Anna did return home it was always a celebrated and welcomed event, as townsfolk were always curious to catch a glimpse of New Annan's most famous citizen.

P. T. Barnum with, from left to right, Commodore Nutt, General Tom Thumb, Lavinia Warren and her sister Minnie Warren. A rivalry developed between Commodore Nutt and General Tom Thumb for the hand of Lavinia Warren, who measured 81 centimetres (32 inches) tall and weighed only 13 kilograms (29 pounds). In the end General Tom Thumb won Lavinia's heart and the couple were married on February 10, 1863. Courtesy of the author.

Chapter 3

Fires at the Museum

A t midday on July 13, 1865, fire broke out in a defective furnace in the cellar of Barnum's American Museum.

Anna was caught on the third floor and overcome by smoke as flames swept through the building. Her frightening predicament was described as follows in a local newspaper:

> There was not a door through which her bulky frame could obtain a passage. It was likewise feared that the stairs would break down even if she should reach them. Her best friend, the living skeleton, stood by her as long as he dared, but then deserted her, while as the heat grew in intensity, the perspiration rolled from her face, in little brooks and rivulets, which pattered musically upon the floor. At length, as a last resort, the employees of the place procured a **lofty derrick**, which

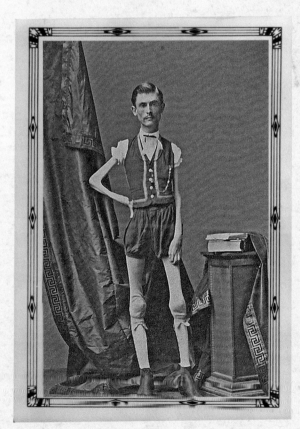

Living Skeleton. Courtesy of Laddy Kite.

fortunately happened to be standing near, and erected it alongside the Museum. A portion of the wall was then broken off on each side of the window, the strong tackle was got in readiness, the fat woman was made fast to one end and swung over the heads of the people in the streets, with eighteen men grasping the other extremity of the line, and lowered down from the third story amid enthusiastic applause. A carriage of extraordinary capacity was in readiness, and, entering this, the young lady was driven away to a hotel.

Burning of Barnum's Museum, July 13, 1865. Courtesy of the New York Public Library Digital Collection.

Having lost her life savings in the fire – along with almost everything she owned – and now without a home, Anna returned to New Annan while Barnum rebuilt his museum.

Although the American Museum was in fact destroyed by fire, it has been questioned if the account of Anna's rescue by derrick actually happened, given that some local newspapers simply stated that Anna left the building without much difficulty. Perhaps the reporter made a mistake and the rescue was of "The Fat Lady," who was also on exhibit at that time at Barnum's museum. Another possibility is that Barnum, who was a master at advertising and often had stories printed in newspapers to help with the promotion of his performers, made up the story of the rescue altogether.

In November 1865, Barnum re-opened at a new location, and Anna sailed back to New York to take her place among the showman's cast of curiosities.

DISASTROUS FIRE.

Total Destruction of Barnum's American Museum.

Nine Other Buildings Burned to the Ground.

LOSS ESTIMATED AT $1,000,000.

The animals during the burning of Barnum's Museum, 1868. Courtesy of the New York Public Library Digital Collection.

However, disaster struck again a few years later when shortly after midnight, on March 3, 1868, fire broke out on the third floor of the new building. As billows of smoke blanketed each floor, animals howled and cowered in the back of their cages, while the museum's human residents frantically tried to find their way to safety. Although police and firemen were quick on the scene, the extreme cold and deep snow made their work all the more difficult.

When morning broke, what remained of Barnum's museum was covered in ice like a giant glacier. Thankfully, no human life was lost, though sadly, many of the animals perished or were injured, as in the fire of 1865.

Exterior of Barnum's Museum after the fire. Courtesy of the New York Public Library Digital Collection.

Anna was interviewed in a local newspaper following the inferno and was reported to have said,

I was in the fourth floor, between the lecture room and the gallery, and it was just about half past twelve, and had got everything off me except my **chemise** and stockings, when I heard a scream – and such a scream! Says I, "Sakes alive, what can that be, I do wonder?" The policemen began to holler; and the fire and smoke came up the stairs into my room. What was a poor woman to do in such a trouble? I was all in a tremor and a flutter, but I grabbed my jewelery ... and, throwing my dress over my shoulders turned to make my way downstairs, with all my portable property in the folds of my dress tucked up; but I did not know where to go, when up came two big policemen with their clubs in their hands and said to me, "Come this way my heavy Old Gal," and I went.

When asked if she was as frightened as she was during the last fire in 1865, Anna then replied, "Sakes alive! young man – I was twice as skeered . You know that was in the daytime and this was in the night – sakes alive, and I had nothing on me but my chemise. What was a poor woman to do?"

Traumatized by the event, Anna returned once again to the family home to recuperate from the ordeal. There, she toured Nova Scotia with a dwarf, measuring 106 centimetres (42 inches) and weighing 18 kilograms (40 pounds), who went by the name of Sir Robert the Bruce. Anna was billed as the "Colchester Giantess," who was 22 years of age, 2.3 metres (7½ feet) tall and weighed 160 kilograms (350 pounds). As part of the show, Anna's waist was measured with a tape, which was then wrapped three times around the waist of a woman from the audience.

It was on one of her return trips to Nova Scotia that Anna was observed shopping for a new hat through a store window. While Anna sat on a chair, onlookers could see a salesgirl standing on a chair behind her to help fit her for a new hat.

On another occasion, a neighbour recounted how Anna, who was visiting their home, sat down at one end of a lounge chair and the opposite end tilted upward like a child's see-saw, so great was her weight. All who observed Anna in such situations noted that though life presented her with many challenges, the gentle giantess met each one with dignity and poise.

Chapter 4

Anna in Love

When not performing at the American Museum, Anna participated in several tours of the United States and Europe. These tours offered Anna the opportunity to travel to faraway cities and countries, an activity that few people could afford to do at that time. As well, during these trips Anna had the good fortune of meeting interesting and, in some cases, famous people – such as the Queen of England herself!

That momentous event occurred in 1863 when Anna toured Europe for the very first time with Barnum. Queen Victoria was quite taken with Anna's charm and grace and enjoyed her company greatly.

Anna participated in several other tours of the United States and Europe after that, including one she undertook in 1869, which lasted eight months. The trip began in Glasgow, Scotland, the homeland of her ancestors. Anna's

Queen Victoria (1819-1901) became the ruler of Great Britain in 1837 at the age of eighteen. Her nearly sixty-four-year reign is the longest in British history. Courtesy Library and Archives Canada / C-001590.

maternal and paternal grandparents were both of Scottish heritage, and she was most interested in finding out as much as she could about her family history.

Edinburgh Evening Courant, February 24, 1869.

Anna then moved on to England, where she gave daily levees at the famous Egyptian Hall in Piccadilly. With the tour completed,

Illustrated Times, March 20, 1869.

Anna returned to New York to Barnum's American Museum. Little did she realize she would soon be crossing the Atlantic once again.

Having fulfilled her latest contract with P. T. Barnum, Anna decided to join the company of Judge H. P. Ingalls, who was organizing a three-year tour of Europe. What made the prospect of this tour so attractive to Anna was the fact that Martin Van Buren Bates, known as the Kentucky Giant, was also part of the troupe. Anna had met Martin at a party some months earlier in New Jersey while touring the United States. In her long letters home, Anna mentioned him frequently, stating how she had found him charming and appealing. The feeling, it appeared, was mutual.

Poster of Anna Swan. Courtesy of the British Library.

The Egyptian Hall. Courtesy of the Wellcome Library.

Martin Van Buren Bates was born November 9, 1837, and was the youngest of the twelve children of John W. and Sarah Bates of Whitesburg, Kentucky. As was the case with Anna's family, Martin's siblings and parents were all of average height. At a young age, Martin showed remarkable growth and had reached nearly 2 metres (6 feet) in height by his 13th birthday. In September 1861 Martin answered the call for volunteers for the American Civil War. He enlisted in the Fifth Kentucky Infantry and rose in rank from private to first lieutenant. When the war ended, Martin decided to join Wiggins and Bennoit, a small circus in Cincinnati, Ohio. From there he joined the John Robinson Circus as "The Kentucky Mountain Giant," then signed with the company of Judge H. P. Ingalls. According to Martin, he continued to grow steadily until he reached his full height of 2.3 metres (7 feet, 8 inches) at age twenty-eight.

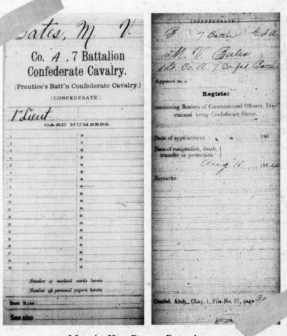

Martin Van Buren Bates's war record. Courtesy of Rhonda Cookenour Turner.

Martin Van Buren Bates enlisted in the Fifth Kentucky Infantry, which disbanded and later merged with the Seventh Confederate Cavalry, Co. Martin was alleged to have carried two enormous pistols made especially for him that he wore strapped across his chest in black leather holsters. His saber was 45 centimetres (18 inches) longer than the standard weapon and he rode a huge Percheron horse. His fame spread among Union soldiers as "That Confederate Giant who was as big as 5 men and fought like 50." Martin claimed to have been promoted to captain and to having served to the end of the war; however, he resigned from the cavalry in August 1864 as a first lieutenant. Martin's war records state, "He is nearly seven feet high and weighs three hundred and fifty pounds. He is not able to perform military duties on foot and there is not a horse in the Confederate States Army to carry him for any length of time."

Martin Van Buren Bates and Judge H. P. Ingalls. Courtesy of Diane Gudatis.

The American Civil War pitted the northern states, known as the Union, against the Confederacy, which were the eleven southern states that wanted to break away from the United States of America. The main reason for the conflict was slavery, which was more accepted in the South than the North. Southern planters relied on slaves to run their **plantations** and make them profitable. Many northerners disagreed with this practice and felt that owning slaves was wrong. The war raged from 1861 until 1865, when the North won. The country remained united and slavery came to an end.

City of Brussels. *Courtesy Keffer Collection of Sheet Music, 1872, Rare Book and Manuscript Library. University of Pennsylvania.*

Monsieur Joseph, the French Giant and a man of average height. Courtesy of the Special Collections, University of Nevada-Reno Library.

As they sailed across the ocean on the *City of Brussels* in April of 1871, Martin and Anna spent much time together, getting to know each other. It therefore came as no surprise to the other members of the company when Martin proposed before the ship had even docked in Liverpool.

This was not Anna's first marriage proposal; she had received a few in previous years, including one from Monsieur Joseph, the French Giant, which she had refused. But true love had now blossomed in Anna's life, and she accepted Martin's proposal with joy.

On the morning of Saturday, June 17, 1871, the church of St. Martin-in-the-Fields in London's Trafalgar Square was brimming with curious onlookers eager to witness the "tall" spectacle of the wedding of Anna Swan (age 24) and Martin Van Buren Bates (33).

According to London newspapers, Martin arrived at exactly a quarter to eleven and walked composedly up to the altar. He did not wear his army uniform, but rather a blue coat and grey trousers. Five minutes later, loud whispers were followed by a dead silence, announcing Anna's arrival at the church door. Dressed in a gown sewn of 100 metres of satin and 50 metres of lace and decorated with embroidered orange blossoms, the giantess moved majestically up the aisle and stood next to her husband-to-be.

The church of St. Martin-in-the-Fields in London, England. Courtesy of the Creamery Square Heritage Centre.

Marriage certificate of Martin Van Buren Bates and Anna Swan. Courtesy of the City of Westminster Archives Centre. (Note how Anna was called a spinster, and Martin was called a bachelor.)

Anna's gown was a gift of Queen Victoria and was reported to have cost $1,000 to make. Courtesy of the Creamery Square Heritage Centre.

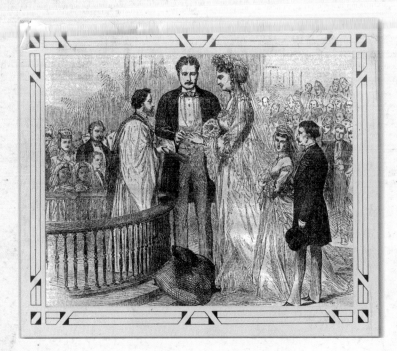

Illustrated London News, June 24, 1871. Courtesy of the Nova Scotia Museum.

Wedding photo of Martin and Anna. Courtesy of the Creamery Square Heritage Centre.

The marriage was performed by Reverend W. Rupert Cochrane, himself a native of Nova Scotia. In attendance were some of Anna and Martin's colleagues, including Millie-Christine, the conjoined twins who went by the stage name, "The Two-Headed Nightingale."

Outside the church, police held back crowds of people to clear a path for the wedding party to reach their awaiting carriages. Following the ceremony, a wedding breakfast was held at the home Anna and Martin had rented, after which the couple left for Richmond to honeymoon at the fashionable Star and Garter Hotel. In describing their accommodations Martin said it was a fine place and that the bill was "as long as his arm."

Mille-Christine. Courtesy of the Wellcome Library.

Star and Garter Hotel. Courtesy of the author.

Upon returning from their honeymoon the couple found an order of the Queen awaiting them, requesting they present themselves at Buckingham Palace. As wedding gifts, the Queen presented Anna with a diamond cluster ring, while Martin received a massive gold watch and chain. The couple appeared again before the Queen on two occasions and were also guests of the Prince of Wales. As well, they gave private levees for numerous other royals, including the Grand Duke Vladimir of Russia and Prince John of Luxembourg. When not mingling with royalty, the couple was on exhibit at a number of theatres and concert halls.

Within a year, Anna became pregnant with the couple's first child, and on March 19, 1872, gave birth to a daughter. The baby weighed 8 kilograms (18 lbs) and measured 69 centimetres (27 inches), but sadly, she died at birth. Anna and Martin were devastated and the loss took a great toll on Anna's health, leaving her weakened and depressed. The couple went into semi-retirement and for the next two years only gave receptions by royal command.

Chapter 5

Settling in Seville

On July 2, 1874, Anna and her husband closed the chapter on their life in Europe and sailed back to North America aboard the *City of Antwerp*. During the next few months, the couple visited the home of Anna's parents to introduce Martin to her family and travelled as tourists throughout the United States. Then, with a view to putting down roots and lead a more stable life, they purchased 52 hectares (130 acres) of land in the farming community of Seville, Ohio.

It is not entirely clear why this particular location appealed to the giants. Perhaps it was the charm of the vast expanses of land and green meadows, the two babbling creeks – Hubbard and Chippewa – that flowed through the town and the rustic bridges that dotted the countryside.

Martin Van Buren Bates, his wife Anna and an unknown person. Courtesy of Matt Swain.

The house Anna and Martin built was large in the front and small at the back, where the servants and houseguests would sleep. The house no longer stands. It was dismantled by the family who purchased the property, and a smaller house was built, using the lumber from the giants' house. Photo courtesy of the Creamery Square Heritage Centre.

Anna's health no doubt played a role in their decision to lead a more tranquil and relaxed existence, as she was still noticeably weakened by the birth and loss of their baby daughter two years earlier and needed to rebuild her strength. And so, Anna and Martin set about building themselves a home, which attracted as much attention as the giants themselves.

The frame construction made of yellow pine consisted of four side-by-side block buildings that held eighteen rooms. The couple resided in the main wing of the farmhouse where ceilings ranged from 3.5 to 4 metres (12 to 14) feet high and doors measured 2.6 metres (8-and-a-half feet) high, each adorned with doorknobs set at the height of an average man's head. No longer did Martin and Anna have to stoop when entering a room, or turn sideways because of narrow door frames.

The ground floor housed a number of rooms, including a dining room, a **parlour**, a living room and a bedroom. The bed in which Anna and Martin slept was 3 metres (10 feet) long and almost as wide. Though normal in size, the piano, which sat in the living room, was mounted on stilts that were a metre (3 feet) high, making it difficult for anyone but

Martin Van Buren Bates, his wife Anna and an unknown person. Courtesy of Matt Swain.

the couple to reach the keys. The living room also included two rocking chairs that visitors climbed into by scaling the rungs, just as a child would climb into a high chair. The dining room table was made of varying heights, extra high at one end and lower at the other, so Anna and Martin could eat their meals with their guests. Rooms were separated by sliding doors panelled in rare woods, and fireplace mantels were adorned with imported marble.

The back portion of the house was used as servants' quarters and had much lower ceilings. Barns were also built for Martin's farm animals, mainly Shorthorn cattle and

Percheron horses that he raised and bred. For travel, the couple had an enormous carriage built, along with a large sleigh for the winter months, both of which were drawn by their Percherons.

The community quickly embraced the shy, gentle giantess and her fiery-tempered husband who, on occasion, was known to quarrel with his neighbours. The couple became devoted members of the Seville First Baptist Church and were regularly seen on Sundays sitting in the extra large pew Martin had built for them. Anna also taught Sunday school to the children and kept busy with various church projects, organizing teas and bazaars and attending quilting parties where the other ladies sat captivated as Anna regaled them with stories of her life with P. T. Barnum and her many tours.

Seville First Baptist Church. Photo courtesy of the Creamery Square Heritage Centre.

The couple were particularly fond of children. Martin played games with the little ones who would climb him, like a mountain, to search his pockets, which he kept full of candy. He also entertained them with the pocket watch given to him by Queen Victoria, which the children held to their ears; they were often lulled to sleep by the soothing ticking.

Chapter 6

Losing Anna

To help pay for the cost of building their farmhouse, Anna and her husband decided to join the W. W. Coles Circus on their 1878 tour. The circus owner boasted having paid $20,000 to secure their appearance and billed them as "The Two Largest People in the World." The giant couple attracted thousands of spectators.

Anna and Martin returned home following the end of the touring season and on January 15, 1879, Dr. A. P. Beach was called to the farm. Anna was in labour. The couple's second child was to be born.

Anna Swan and Martin Van Buren Bates had a combined height of more than 4.5 metres (15 feet) and a total weight of nearly 363 kilograms (800 pounds). Courtesy of Marc Hartzman.

Anna remained in labour for another three days until finally on January 19 she gave birth to the largest baby known to medical history. Weighing nearly 11 kilograms (23 ¾ pounds) and measuring 76 centimetres (30 inches) in length, the baby boy only lived approximately eleven hours.

Anna and Martin were once again devastated by the loss.

Anna's bouts of fatigue continued to plague her, so the couple decided to retire following the circus's 1880 tour. Back in Seville, they went on with their peaceful and productive lives. All the while Martin took care of the farm and was also supportive of many town projects.

The couple's home remained a popular haven for the many friends they had made throughout the years who visited on occasion, including the Siamese twins, Millie-Christine, who had attended their wedding in England, and Lavinia Warren, also known as Mrs. Tom Thumb. Townsfolk would mistake her for a doll riding in the giants' carriage whenever she came to visit. The giants' household was also home to many pets, the most popular being Anna's monkey, Button.

Although it was clear to Martin that Anna's health was failing, it still came as a great shock to him when she died suddenly at their home on August 5, 1888, the eve of her forty-second birthday. Heart failure was said to be the reason for her unexpected death.

Over the years the small community of Seville had grown quite fond of the kind-hearted giantess, and news of her death was met with great sorrow.

In her last will and testament, Anna, who had always helped her family financially as much as she could, left generous sums of money to her parents and siblings. Her parents each received $500, while her five surviving brothers and sisters each received $1,502.25.

Following Anna's death, Martin placed an order for Anna's casket with a Cleveland coffin maker who, believing he had been given the wrong dimensions, sent a regular-sized casket to the farm. Anna's burial was delayed for three days, the time taken to have a proper-sized casket built for her. To avoid the same mistake being repeated when the time came for his own burial, Martin later had a casket built for himself, which he stored in his barn.

Anna's funeral was scheduled for August 8, which also gave her parents enough time to travel the three days and three nights by train from Nova Scotia. According to the *Seville*

Summary of Anna's estate. Courtesy of the Creamery Square Heritage Centre.

Times, the couple's home was too small to contain everyone, so great were the number of friends and family members in attendance at Anna's funeral.

The spacious house being too straight to hold them, the services, necessarily brief, were held on the veranda, the people sitting and standing in the yard. The procession of carriages which followed the remains to their last resting place extended over the whole distance lying between the house and the cemetery.

Martin had a statue made in Anna's likeness, to stand above her grave. Although the monument was meant to measure nearly 5 metres (16 feet) in height, a 10 centimetres (six-inch) section from the waist was lost when the statue was shipped from England. Martin was so enraged by this when the monument was uncrated at the cemetery that he had to be escorted home.

Tombstone of Anna Swan and Martin Van Buren Bates. Photo courtesy of the Creamery Square Heritage Centre.

Martin Van Buren Bates and Frank Bowman, a midget who lived in nearby Medina. Photo courtesy of Steve DeGenaro.

Martin Van Buren Bates with his second wife, Lavonne, and Frank Bowman. Photo courtesy of Steve DeGenaro.

Marriage licence of Martin Van Buren Bates and Lavonne Weatherby. Courtesy of Rhonda Cookenour Turner.

On October 23, 1889, Martin married again, this time to an average-sized woman, Lavonne Weatherby. Because of his new wife's diminutive size, Martin moved out of the house he had built for himself and Anna, into an average-sized house where he lived until his death in 1919, at the age of 81.

On January 10, 1919, Martin Van Buren Bates was buried alongside his beloved Anna and their baby son at the Mound Hill Cemetery.

The last house Martin Van Buren Bates lived in, with his second wife. Photo courtesy of the Creamery Square Heritage Centre.

Chapter 7

Legacy

Today, both Anna and her husband Martin Van Buren Bates are fondly remembered in Seville, Ohio. Visitors to the area are met by a road sign commemorating the couple's life there. In addition, the town holds an annual Giant Fest, which highlights the lives of the world's tallest married couple.

Road sign in Seville Ohio. Photo courtesy of the Creamery Square Heritage Centre.

Artifacts are showcased at the Seville Historical Museum, including a model of their house and the cradle which had been built for Anna and Martin's second child. Replicas of clothing items and of Martin's ring, which is an amazing size 22, are also on display.

Although their house no longer stands, having been dismantled in 1948, the barn does, and still bears the words "Capt. M. V. Bates" on the roof.

Anna Swan's legacy is also lovingly preserved and nurtured in Colchester County, Nova Scotia.

Visitors to the region can view a monument that stands close to the home where Anna's family once lived. The inscription reads as follows:

The barn of Martin Van Buren Bates, which still stands today. Photo courtesy of the Creamery Square Heritage Centre.

> Anna Haining Swan was born at Millbrook Colchester Co., N.S., on August 6, 1846. When Anna was three years old the family moved to Central New Annan. At 17 years of age she was 7 feet 11½ inches tall and weighed 413 lbs, and attracted the interest of showman Phineas T. Barnum. She was billed as "The tallest girl in the world" at his American Museum on Broadway, and she later travelled throughout America and Europe, where she was received by Queen Victoria. She married Martin Van Buren Bates in 1871 and died in Seville, Ohio, in 1888.

As well, in the village of Tatamagouche, home to the Creamery Square Heritage Centre, visitors can view artifacts of Anna's life and learn more about the loving, kind-hearted giantess who touched the lives of many with her grace, dignity and compassion.

Hailed as the pride of Nova Scotia, Anna continues to be acclaimed as a woman who, despite her unusual and challenging physical attributes, rose above adversity to lead a life of love, happiness and adventure.

ANNA SWAN BATES
NOVA SCOTIA GIANTESS

ANNA HAINING SWAN WAS BORN AT MILLBROOK, COLCHESTER Co., N.S.
ON AUGUST 6, 1846. WHEN ANNA WAS THREE YEARS OLD THE FAMILY
MOVED TO CENTRAL NEW ANNAN. AT 17 YEARS OF AGE SHE WAS 7 FEET
11½ INCHES TALL AND WEIGHED 413 LBS., AND ATTRACTED THE INTEREST
OF SHOWMAN PHINEAS T. BARNUM. SHE WAS BILLED AS "THE TALLEST GIRL
IN THE WORLD" AT HIS AMERICAN MUSEUM ON BROADWAY, AND SHE LATER
TRAVELLED THROUGHOUT AMERICA AND EUROPE, WHERE SHE WAS RECEIVED
BY QUEEN VICTORIA. SHE MARRIED MARTIN VAN BUREN BATES IN
1871 IN LONDON AND DIED IN SEVILLE, OHIO, IN 1888.

Plaque in remembrance of Anna Swan Bates near Tatamagouche, Nova Scotia. Photo courtesy of the Creamery Square Heritage Centre.

Creamery Square Heritage Centre. Photo courtesy of the Creamery Square Heritage Centre.

Timeline:

August 6, 1846   Anna Swan is born in Millbrook, Nova Scotia.

March 1851   Anna's first tour of Nova Scotia as the "Infant Giantess."

September 1861   Anna attends Normal School in Truro.

August 1862   Anna joins Barnum's American Museum.

July 13, 1865   American Museum is destroyed by fire.

March 3, 1868   American Museum is again destroyed by fire.

November 1870   Anna meets Martin Van Buren in New Jersey.

April 1871   Anna and Martin sail to Europe with H. P. Ingalls's troupe.

June 17, 1871   Anna Swan and Martin Van Buren Bates are married in London, England.

May 19, 1872   Anna and Martin's daughter is born in London.

July 2, 1874   Anna and Martin leave Europe and return to the United States.

January 19, 1879   Anna and Martin's son is born.

August 5, 1888   Anna Swan Bates dies in Seville, Ohio.

October 23, 1889   Martin marries Lavonne Weatherby.

January 7, 1919   Martin Van Buren Bates dies in Ohio.

Lexicon

chamber pot: A round container used in a bedroom as a toilet.

chaperone: An older or married woman who supervises or accompanies a young unmarried woman, especially at social events.

chemise: A woman's loose, shirt-like undergarment or nightdress.

contortionist: A performer who twists and bends his body into strange and unusual positions for the entertainment of others.

daftie: An Old English word that means someone who is a slow learner or mentally challenged.

derrick: Equipment for hoisting and swinging great weights.

goitre: A swelling at the front of the neck that is due to an enlarged thyroid gland. The thyroid gland stores hormones that help regulate many things in our body, including our growth.

levee: A formal reception of visitors or guests.

lofty: To extend high in the air, or be of an imposing height.

Normal School: A Normal School was a school that trained people to become teachers, generally for the primary grades. Today these schools are called teachers' colleges.

parlour: A small sitting room where visitors were entertained.

plantation: A large farm or estate, on which food crops are grown, such as cotton, tobacco, sugar cane and coffee.

Quaker:

Quakerism is a Christian movement that was founded in England in the mid-17th century. Its followers call themselves "Friends." Their formal title is "The Religious Society of Friends (Quakers)." Quakers believe that each individual is directly responsible to God, so they have no priests or pastors and no religious ceremonies. Quakers tend to live simply and practise non-violence and forgiveness. Most Quakers refuse to fight in wars.

tableaux:

A living picture or "photograph," where people are perfectly still and posed in a way to convey a moment, or scene.

tutor:

A private teacher who gives individual instruction to another person on one or more subjects.

Bibliography

Books

Bates, Martin Van Buren. *A Historical Sketch of the Tallest Man and Wife that Has Ever Existed, Captain Martin Van Buren Bates and Mrs. Bates, Formerly Anna Swan: Together with a Short Description of Mythological, Ancient, Medevial [sic] and Modern Giants.* New York: New York Popular Publishing Company, 1880.

Blakeley, Phyllis R. *Nova Scotia's Two Remarkable Giants.* Hantsport, NS: Lancelot Press, 1970.

Cavin, Lee. *There were Giants on the Earth!* Seville, OH: Seville Chronicle Press, 1959.

Fitzsimons, Raymond. *Barnum in London.* London: Geoffrey Bles Ltd., 1969.

Giles Millard, Ellen. *Big Annie: The Nova Scotian Giantess.* The Colchester Printing Company, 2008.

Holt Gramly, Allene. *The World's Tallest Couple: Biographical Novel.* Mansfield, OH: Appleseed Press, 1983.

Langille, Jacqueline. *Giants Angus McAskill and Anna Swan.* Tantallon, NS: Four East Publications Ltd., 1990.

Lee, Polly Jae. *Giant: The Pictorial History of the Human Colosssus.* New York: A.S. Barnes and Company, 1970.

Vacon, Shirley Irene. *Giants of Nova Scotia: The Lives of Anna Swan and Angus McAskill.* East Lawrencetown, NS: Pottersfield Press, 2008.

Magazine Articles

Burrows, Mary. "Anna Swan: Nova Scotia's Famed Giantess." *Chatelaine Magazine,* December 1966.

Kindig, Eileen Silva. "Giants of Seville." *Western Reserve Magazine,* September/October 1977.

Mann, Charlotte. "The Seville Giants: They Had A Big Thing Going." *Western Reserve Magazine,* July/August 1982.

Burden, George. "The giantess of Nova Scotia." *The Medical Post,* March 3, 1998.

Newspapers

The Nova Scotian, July 14, 1851.

The New York Times, January 26, 1864.

The New York Times, July 14, 1865.

The Daily Index (Petersburg, Virginia), July 17, 1865.

Harper's Weekly, July 29, 1865.

Adams Sentinel (Gettysburg, Pennsylvania), August 18, 1865.

Waukeska Plaindealer (Waukeska, Wisconsin), March 17, 1868.

The New York Times, February 2, 1869.
Edinburgh Evening Courant, February 24, 1860.
Illustrated Times, March 20, 1869.
The Non-Conformist (Middlesex, London), June 21, 1871.
Illustrated London News, June 24, 1871.
Week's News (London, Middlesex) June 24, 1871.
The Greenville Advance Argus (Greenville, Pennsylvania), August 15, 1878.
Petersburg Index-Appeal (Petersburg, Virginia), September 14, 1878.
Weekly Graphic (Kirksville, Adair Co., Missouri), March 17, 1882.
Daily Globe (St. Paul Minnesota), July 22, 1883.
The Seville Times, August 5, 1888.
Richmond Dispatch (Richmond, Virginia), December 2, 1894.
The New York Times, March 11, 1896.

Interviews
Dale Swan, great grand-nephew of Anna Swan.
Rhonda Cookenour Turner, 3rd great grand-niece of Martin Van
    Buren Bates.

About the Author

Anne Renaud is a life-long Quebecker. She received her Bachelor of Translation from Concordia University in Montreal.

Anne is the author of several picture books, as well as historical non-fiction books for children, including, *A Bloom of Friendship: The Story of the Canadian Tulip Festival*, *Island of Hope and Sorrow: The Story of Grosse Île*, *Into the Mist: The Story of the Empress of Ireland* and *Pier 21: Stories from Near and Far* (to be re-released by CBU Press in 2014). Her work has been nominated for several awards, including the Silver Birch Award, the Hackmatack Children's Choice Award, the Red Cedar Book Award, the Red Maple Award and the Quebec Writers' Federation Prize for Children's & Young Adult Literature. She was selected as a touring author for TD Canadian Children's Book Week (2013).

Anne is also a regular contributor to children's magazines, such as *Highlights*, *Pockets*, *Cricket*, *Odyssey*, *Faces*, *Clubhouse* and *Shine*.

Anne's readers often ask her why she writes books. She tells them it is because she likes to do creative things and she finds writing to be a very creative exercise. It's also because she can't dance well and she can't sing well, so she tries her best at writing well. She hopes her books educate, entertain and inspire children.